LIFE SENTENCES

Published by Molonglo Press
PO Box 1283
Woden ACT 2606
Australia

Telephone: (02) 6260 4555
Facsimile: (02) 6260 4499
E-mail: pubs@molonglo.com.au
Website: www.molonglo.com.au

National Library of Australia Cataloguing-in-Publication data

Caesar, Adrian, 1955– .
        Life sentences.

        ISBN 1 876827 01 7.

        I. Title.

A821.3

Cover illustration by Romola Templeman
Designed and produced by Molonglo Press
Printed by Goanna Print, Canberra

LIFE SENTENCES

ADRIAN CAESAR

MOLONGLO
PRESS

ACKNOWLEDGEMENTS

I would like to thank the editors of the following publications in which some of these poems have previously appeared: *Canberra Times, Canberra Review, Critical Survey* (UK), *Famous Reporter, Muse, National Library of Australia News, Southerly, Voices.*

Molonglo Press thanks Heather and John Seymour, whose generous assistance made the publication of this book possible, and Phil Abbott of Goanna Print for his enthusiastic support.

This project has been assisted by the Commonwealth Government through the Australia Council, its arts funding and advisory body.

CONTENTS

LUGGAGE HANDLING

A room has no nation
it could be anywhere
the night before leaving
either here or there,
the open suitcase on the bed
Mum and Dad trying to help
fussing as to how to keep
their fragile gifts
this cup, that plate, intact
by wrapping them in socks and jocks.

Then my emigrant distress—
how all my life will not fit in
no matter what I do
I'm forever bouncing on the lid,
risking smash and spill
and when I lug it to the scales
my baggage is always in excess.

LANDSCAPES

When I was young
I didn't think of countryside,
saw not felt how beautiful it was,
those constricted acres
neat hedges and tiny fields
decorated with friesian heifers
were a foreign language,
it was the property still of
aristocrats, not for the likes
of a suburban townie
from St Helens, the only place
my sister said, where brewery
and church were indistinguishable:
square, red-brick monstrosities
serving roughly the same purpose.
No, despite my parents'
upward push, my sensibility
was honed on pavements
where rags of wind-blown
chip-papers tumbled through rows
of terraced houses and landscape was
factory chimney and winding gear,
the canal by Pilkington's steaming
whilst hopeful fishermen
sat facing that blank wall
hoping for tropical fish
some said the effluent encouraged.

Then to Australia and the great spaces
of bush and sea and sky; the mind
at first, stretching, then relaxed
each new and massive landscape
a figure of escape, a place at last
I told myself that I could call familiar,
a boundless wilderness in which
to set imagination free.
But recently camping at Wirraweena
climbing those ancient ranges
where the wedge-tailed eagle haunts
the thermals, or exploring creek-beds
beneath the cathedral vaulting
of red and river gums, listening
to a friend explain the Aboriginal
and settler history of the place,
I am an intruder once again
as if one can't cut off the past
of colony and empire with neat saws:
'you can't inherit guilt,' I've told
myself a thousand times, but
when I hear the Adnyamathanha
have been mining ochre hereabouts
for thirty thousand years,
I'm put in my stranger place,
returning to suburbia
try to know more nearly where it is
I both belong and don't.

THE GIFT

Visiting parents from another world
I'm asked to sort books that were mine as a child;
the *Treasure Island* I read when I was six
football annuals, *Observer's* volumes
of keenly ogled planes and ships.

They remind me how, in my mother's words,
I was a real little boy or tried so hard to be,
climbing trees with the Marshall's gang
it was all bloody noses and scratched knees
I scored my first league goal at eight.

Somehow sport, adventure, travel became me
'stop reading that poofter poetry and come
play footy' was the cry at school and when
unemployment beckoned I made myself
a romantic migrant, business class by Jumbo jet.

But now the thirty-six hour flight is just
another boozy haul, approaching forty
my last game beckons and island treasure
is buried beyond reach forever. So these
childhood imprints are packed nostalgia

for a jumble sale, my past in carrier bags
to please some random boy who may perfect
a climb through branches or dumb cloud
to risk by tree or plane those artful heights
where dizzying words change people and incite.

CAMBRIDGE 1994

This city of bells
chimes like a Betjeman poem
girls on old-fashioned cycles
baskets stuffed with racquets
hair, dress and accent
a blue-ribbon privilege,
move past architecture
still magnificent, still just about
the best of British ...

But this is Orwell plus ten.
At night in doorways
beggars with dogs
lie vomit-stained,
they hurl crushed cans
at black-tied youth on its way
to formals dreaming of that girl
who says 'super', 'marvellous' as
she twists dark hair into blue bows.

And the coins these lovers throw
between two Englands
precludes discussion
of their common heritage
disarms the plot for a future state
of democratic grace.
And the old bells summon
their praying devotees
indifferent to the rest.

SONGS

for Mum

Before school began my long unlearning
after dinner, which was lunch up North,
my Mum would hold me on the table
and sing about a cat whose tail caught fire
and burnt down the house:
Ding-dong derrio let's all be merrio
Little boy, pretty boy, under the broom.

Or there was one concerning
the return of some errant prodigal
met by neighbours, kissing the Collins' all.
He was embraced by sister Kate
and even the girl he used to swing
down by the garden gate declared him
welcome as the flowers in May to dear old Donegal.

Those strange words sank into me
forming strange flotsam in seas of loss
which now I daily cruise
as if in that divided stream I first
became enmeshed in gentle nets of art,
both trawler and traveller
knowing that as a voyage is long
so the greeting's great when the ship comes in.

My first day at school I was chastised
for singing. I wanted to set the world
on fire. Ever since I've been writing
my journey, hoping for others to be
enflamed by these burning tales;
trying to bring the house down,
always I crave the large reception
my ear tuned to the rhythm of the swing
that lost girl waving by the garden's gate.

CHRISTMAS PAST

I'm lost again
in that old country of romance
the squat towered Norman church
at Froda's Ham, Christmas Eve,
illumined by snowfall at midnight
I am a choir boy aged thirteen
trudging by the graveyard wall
having been to a party where
spin-the-bottle had allowed
my tongue first to twist
in the subtle invention of a kiss.
The smell of dust mingles
with incense and candle flame
as we process clothed in illusion
scarlet cassocks, white surplices
mime purity and passion
following the golden cross.
And then a boy's voice (not mine)
arced to stone spaces
the most worldly rendered dumb
as his angelic treble figured
human aspiration, disembodied,
rising to make for a moment:
a magical love, peace on earth,
goodwill etc, a painless nativity.

For the choir girl,
dark hair tumbling,
who did not think of me
her grey eyes beautiful in grief
I was tempted to prayer.
Leaving church my lips were touched
with snowflakes. I wanted to make
desire part of this village idyll
but was left with bottles
their empty spin seeming to confer,
like our cold hands at parting,
these gleanings of winter,
a talent for random sadness.

CHRISTMAS PRESENT

Awake to the smell of frost
eyelids gummed with cold
conjures when I was a lad
there were icy patterns
on the inside of each pane
and mum would bathe my eyes awake
with cotton wool and songs.

Now with winter in July
abroad I live in comfort
with the morning freeze.
Hot water touches insight;
I sing christmas carols
in the shower and dream
of christmas trees.

Then driving home at night
under the glaze of frost and moon
I see three camels graze
the stony acre, imagine
bushmen kings who sing
hard yakka, shickered to heaven
following their practical star.

And so between hemispheres
I find the feast is moveable
and mythologies always need
to be re-written. There is no
salvation from crucifixion
and okker sentiment is a blind
for brusque brutality.

Though we begin and end in winter
and each hard dawn and dusk
finds our open eyes unstuck
staring at the chilly facts,
nativity instinct with grief and loss;
still I sing these marginal hymns
find praise in a window's patterning.

THE TRESPASSER

for Syd Harrex

'All poetry is trespass', you said
so I leapt over your fence with words
into the fields of youth again
where I heard tweed-suited parody

a gamekeeper, gun crooked over arm,
with the inevitable labrador
'Hey you, stop, do you know
whose land you're walking on?'

Cocky I said, 'Lord Pilkington's
and this is right-of-way not crops.'
'No this 'ere's Lord Derby land
and you're a trespasser,' he said,

'Don't let me see you 'ere again
or the police'll have you next time.'
My mouth zipped anger in forever—
fields and trees were not for me

but the sherry set with landrovers,
and I thought of Nan at twelve leaving school
for the Mill and Will her husband
volunteering for trenches.

Lord Derby's scheme approved of that
and other kinds of sacrifice
no wonder as a man I left to seek
this 'paradise' for the working class

where now I find I'm on another's land again
but ask no leave from the dispossessed
to enjoy my suburban ownership
this quarter acre block

and do not see slaughter in deserts
the hanging prisoners in their cells
or hear the last croaks of a dying tongue
saying take me back to my own land

but instead inscribe in black
this frail apology of verse—
a hope that some day we might agree
to allow all people trespass.

Though schooled on Merseyside
my accent isn't scouse.
I never lived in Liverpool,
but still the city draws me
to its waterfront
a perennial migrant
bidding farewell to Hope Street
its two cathedrals, my faith
in the crown of thorns and slab
of conscience unravelling
as the river's grey swathe
stretches towards the Antipodes.
In funerary light, a watery sun
yellows the sky's contusions.
The docks harbour my invented past.
I am preparing to sail again.

It is a place of strange inheritance
and holds my father's recurring dream.
He's wandering the old dock road alone
past forests of masts and blood-house pubs.
Liverpool Judies nod and beckon
towards a maze of gutted buildings.
He is lost, looking for home.

When I was a child we stood together
by the derelict dock its grim
rectangular silence like smashed windows
giving on darkness. In bombed warehouses

I stood and felt violent ghosts clutch
threatening with past commerce
to anchor me in loss forever.

So I slipped my father's hand
to escape the homeless dream and take
another tide, a latter-day emigrant
leaving relatives with stores of loneliness
they press damp rags to eyes of blank waters
while I load treasured memories,
write my free passage out.

Streets of violence were the place
of my first song. Sixteen, I'd seen
a bovver boy beat up a street vendor.
I rushed past on the other side.
On the last bus home, frightened,
I first created melody from other
people's misery. The unshaded light-
bulb in the window spoke the acme
of neglect; comfortless rooms were
fine material, where arms of struggle
cradle fury, and love is a muddle
of fists and regret, there you'll find
rich pickings for the bourgeois poet.
And as the city dropped behind I heard
the sirens sounding: leave it, leave it.

I am building a port
for imagination to depart from.
I am unloading nostalgia
onto quays of grief.
I am in dry dock
where untidy accretions
of the past are scraped clean.
I am refitting
for another voyage.

Unlike those earlier immigrants
their farewell to England a dream
of past and future as long and wide
as the river that took them,
I can and keep returning. They plunged
slowly towards a space they could
only fill as utopia, eldorado
or a hell of loss and terror,
while with every passing mile
the acres and cities of oppression
seemed kinder, relatives more beloved.
Some for their sanity became artists
of diary and letter setting their words
sail in both directions, life sentences
making the voyage whole.

Suburbs are neither heaven nor hell
the doldrums comfortable in mid-passage,
jetting between Canberra and Merseyside
it's easy to forget one day the trip
for all of us will be one way, a final
embarkation to the land of no return;
our last imagination an Edenic idyll
or night-terror nothingness.
And what will be left are these poor
testaments, the last scratches of will;
steering between waves of sentiment
and the solitary isles of narcissus
towards unstable resolution,
is it too much to ask that when I've done
you'll take my ashes back and on a day of
grey washed cloud and shrieking gull
scatter me into metaphor on the Mersey's tide?
Tugged both ways, let me sail my last journey
home again from home.

AT THE PHOENIX BAR

In Irish pubs the jigs and reels
of the blood; I'm back dancing
Guinness tanked towards a false
denouement in your youthful bed.

I wrote a poem on your thigh;
a callow felt tip followed tongue's
desire to trace the warmth and sweat
of flesh, outline a carnal artistry.

Twenty years and worlds apart
how surprised you'd be that I
remember now, how sexless we
lay in each other's arms that night

and though my words were washed from you
by the morning's indifferent shower,
your body cleansed of me forever
your departure silent as a kiss

it seems we are made from such affairs,
these casual inscriptions that don't fade
while mind is moved to dance,
felt-tipped tongues still long to touch.

THE FIRE-LIGHTER

for Dad

Monastery cold those childhood mornings
patterned frost on the inside of each pane,
my dad kneeling at his morning orison.
I'd watch his hands busy with newsprint
rolling the double sheet into long tapers
before tying them to knotted wreaths—
the pyre's foundation. On went coal
out came *Swan Vestas* and with a crackle
there was flame. We'd kneel together
hands to the miracle, then he'd be off
to fettle tea and take it for Mum, not knowing
what service he gave in proving love's ritual,
such reverence and thankless care,
in the lighting of fires, his daily making
essential warmth from words that burn.

If I said my love
was defined by midnight rain
against the window
I might be misunderstood—

the sleepless cold and wet
haunting separations
would make an uncomfortable
metaphoric bed.

Yet it is most like home
curled to her flank, listening,
to the drench and wash
of some night storm

the passionate drops
refreshing, cold, and fertile
that remind of how our tears
have seeded a loving ground

or how words skittering
against implacable pains
somehow reassure despite
their disappearance into air

and make me think
there is nothing more to praise
than this our breathing poem
you and I falling together, apart.

KEEPSAKE

for Ellen

That morning we paid at Wordsworth's place
the day before had seen the wintry lake
filmed to become some misty Avalon
enpurpled by a trick of cloud and sun.

All this was prelude to an afternoon
shopping for trinkets in a chilly town
where stone-wall people match their houses
facing choked streets with dull frowns.

At Bowness in the day's last light
I joked I saw the visionary gleam
thinking I'd seen a golden swan
gilded by miracle from cracked clouds.

It was an orange marker buoy with gull.
Yet, my daughter said, 'it's still a poem'.
In the century's last years I stood entranced
that sharp, her unclouded eye could see

beyond souvenirs, video tours, cash exchange,
that transformation's marginal possibility.

Walking across tarmac you turned
to see if I was watching, but
I'd already moved behind dark glass.
You almost shrugged thinking
perhaps of me striding towards
the car and work unwilling to
protract the uneasy process of goodbye.

In that missed glance I felt a loss
like a sentence at cross-purposes,
the missed appointment or row by voice-mail;
a panic of extended fingers that stretch
across some cruel abyss but never reach
their desired, desiring grasp.

I'm writing to say how unspeakable
if our last parting should be like this;
a terrible fixing of what if; a broken
landing on the unforgiving rocks
of perpetual remorse; an undying
echo in the silent chasm of despair.

For now the only way to rest
is to construct your blithe return
me moving beyond smoked glass
to see you clearly walk towards
this happy terminus, our eyes
arms and transport all meeting.

THE INSOMNIAC BUILDER

In the night of doubt and sorrow
lover, love me more,
but love will not be commanded
simply slams the door.

Like a child who terrified
stands outside his parents' room
hears the cries of love exulting
turns back to bed still insecure,

he lies and lets the mind's black weather
weep down the windows rattle and storm,
breaching the walls of all self's surety
engulfed he shivers longs for dawn.

Through curtain's tear spreads morning chorus
he curls to her warmth becomes aware,
speaking like day they must re-assemble
singular patterns of I am, I dare.

In the light of doubt and sorrow
lover teach me more
of how to know love's limitation
build strong walls and open doors.

THE LOOK OF LOVE

If I were a painter I'd daub
my love, your naked form
face down upon the midnight
sheets, your head resting
upon an abandoned arm
your face turned from me.
There I'd brush the contours
of passion and compassion
seeking to cradle your sorrow
with this poor artfulness
that can only stand and stare
as you walk down corridors
of loss where each broken
syllable of farewell echoes
from bright tiles and steel
all your most dear in death
leaving you, woman, beyond words.

And on this canvas no extraneous
cleverness, or decoration
just my dancing hands
struggle with dark hair atumble
that shallow valley of spine
leading to rounded promises
then an elegance of legs,
the pathos of plump toes.

I remember the effort
of speech as I stood transfixed
at the bedroom door, wanting
to articulate seduction:
'if I were a painter, I'd paint you'
meaning this physical sway,
such careful strokes as if
to say I don't need you to turn
with forgiveness for this act
of taking, as I praise,
I know·you exist beyond
the language of this lover's gaze.

TWENTY YEARS ON

It is time at last to speak of you
departed lover, strict thief
who haunts my waking and my sleep—

how lustily we climbed
those attic stairs, inhaling
the smell of straw and dust
while through the skylight
stars clothed our nakedness,
perfectly romantic;

of how somehow I wouldn't do
out of my class, too young,
my art not practised, unequal to you,
and how we paced through grief,
until I saw your disappearing face

etched forever behind the
train's departing glass
smeared with tears.

But I still hear and see you
seated in the fading light
of an English summer
playing a foreign country
Beethoven's moonlight
disappearing note by note
as I try to hold you
but you go stealing
my youth's adagio
a last diminishment

before gently pressed keys
lock the past in place
and for the last time
I leave by the attic stair
glancing behind see the closed door,

you are not there,
I can't return
an older melody moves me on.

STREET CAFE

How the poem
might join
or separate us

you with your
busy occupations
the health department etc

and me
only interested
in disease.

The uselessness
might strike you
and the ego

dedicating yourself
to service
others' needs

whilst I
whatever that is
find here

the ultimate
not me
but something

that can't be measured—
my productivity
is appalling

and quite beyond
sound management
practices.

So in the end
it all comes down
to making this

a place of congenial
meeting
a cafe perhaps

where I offer
intimate chatter
scented by cappuccino

bitter black
but frothy
sweetened by chocolate

a whispering glance
at the characters
that pass by

a cure-all
for boredom
and for love.

NIGHT OF THE MESSAGE

Usurping your sadness
I imagine the drive through fields
scythed by a belligerent moon,
passing the mines of heritage
are you comforted as you go
by the opera on the radio?
Or as you approach his destination
do you ponder how anything
could be said more devastating
than 'he's not dead, but
gripped in limbo, right side gone
he knows no one, his speech
declined to the ringing tones
of silence. If you say "hello darling"
he'll open his eyes and not see you.'

Terror is where we arrive at,
there we are all struck dumb
each garrulous salesman stopped
by this still advertisement of death,
capable of messages that beggar words.

I'm listening to *Don Giovanni,* love,
how the dark statue comes to life
wreaking vengeance while some scant
buffoon chortles a lightsome tune.
Spectator at the catastrophe, I play,
willing the comic resolution.
Remember how we planned champagne
tonight to bless our demotic harmony?

Mere bubbles. Burst
with the entrance of some dark
acidic guest, prating deathly news.
Then articulation founders
silences spread like separations—
you by your father's bed, hoping
for once he might go gentle—
while I take advantage of your tears
balancing on the raw edge of speech
I test abstractions against discord
the 'courage' and 'forgiveness'
we all might have need of one day:
stones in the mouth to those who hunger,
those who thirst.

THE DIE HARD

They call it the passion
this crucifixion of a man
defining love, we're told,

which is to say,
presumably, that desire,
the unruly ache

for an entanglement
of needing limbs
to embrace in the rhythm

of the oldest dance
must be subdued
by dark vows or booze.

Thus romance becomes
an impossible dream,
reality a cold magazine;

there's nowhere to go
that doesn't shriek
betrayal, the trap

is quite precise
kisses in the garden
lead to this

daily denial, each morning
resurrection a reminder
to love without sex

is to inhabit
hell's inner suburbs
a polite Gethsemane.

So the young priest
makes his final bow
at the altar

rail of his obsession,
he needs no Roman soldier
with the nails

to hammer home
the pointlessness
of sacrifice,

and she will never know
but read of a
faithless suicide

the torso by the tracks
a tabloid scandal
a town's dismemberment

as the severed promise
of his life is
soon forgotten

while he exchanges
a hell that is
for one that isn't.

These were the best parental gifts of all
the kitchen knives I daily use
and everyday as if ordained
I think of you, the coins you gave
so that our ties should not be severed
with these tempered blades.

What more appropriate gift for us
who know love's keen serrations?
Yet without this cleaving
how could we renew and feed
our endless hungers once again
turn sharp need to gifts of stinging steel?

THE WIDOW'S STORY

I have come to this cold house above the sea
a wintry seclusion to nurse a treasured grief.
I light the tide wood hugging stone memories,
as once I held his body by the flames.
Now there's no warmth. I can't love myself.
The bed a white ache of emptiness beckons
narrow as a penance. My fingers freeze.
I listen to the ocean inexorable as time
marking its slow erasures, my childish castle
those grown up steps, my lover's face, all gone.
And in the night visitations: through puddles
features I know and do not know dissemble
grief and mirth as at some hideous funfare
trapped in the hall of mirrors, frightened,
guilty at my fear, I long to see him whole.
Awake at 3am the unwanted thoughts begin
is it really him I miss or some invention
a kinetic sculpture of entwining limbs?
Was passion dying in the arms of habit?
We had not made love for weeks before he died.
Yet he went to the boat he'd named for me
that morning singing. A change was on its way
he said, but he'd be back before the squall.
He left me alone to weather the storm.
But now like the wreckage of his boat I'm
beached and broken. I wish for someone
to gather me, set me on fire.

GULL

Temperamental, cantankerous at home
once the boon companion of the pubs
prince of salesmen he could sell himself
pitch a voice above the squabble and chat
the product didn't matter only art
and after such success
hat flung to the hat stand
James Bond of the quick commission
to his money penny wife
the easy tongue of flatter and slash
in a straight suit
tossing between charm and violence.

Regard him now at seventy
standing on some scruffy promontory
not unlike the gulls he's come to feed
thin legs, distended belly
and a hunger that's only become more difficult.
He scatters bread
staring at the estuary feeling the ebb tide pull
and calls to dopey the gull
who is always slow like he is now
who never gets a morsel
whose voice is never heard.

SLOUCH

These days I'm polished on parade
friend to officers and men
I'm touched by salutes that never
were supposed to happen. I've
become posh, almost refined,
I shade professors of the military mind.

It wasn't like that in the old days
I was dusty rough and ready
fighting the Empire's wars
men cleaned their bloody bayonets
on me, I fanned a circle of flies
to reveal a face no one could recognise.

I saved a man from sun and kept
him warm at night; I carried water
to a dying mate. Sometimes I deserted
independent, or hid the mourning tears
of martyrs to the broken shell.
Sometimes I connived at slaughter.

But now I'm dignified and formal
drilled in English my creases sharp
in the name of professionalism
they twist the meaning of my name
until I feel wrong-headed and long
to be bashed into the future's shape.

In my 42nd year I felt my age
all my fathers foundered with feet of clay,
no woman would mother me again,
my daughter left for romance on the stage.

And I saw the last vestiges of idealism
shattered as a girl's body plunged from
the high rise, and narcissus ruled
in the venal parliaments of work and sport

it was goodbye to old selves who'd found
comfort in scoring goals, masculine
chatter, booze and cigarettes, the legs
no longer holding, the career gone

tackled by the sight of professionals
kicking only financial goals the game
pure business, marketing the tawdry
fashions that lead to monstrous fame.

And I stared for the first time at death,
although the word had always stalked me,
now in an old woman's caved-in face
her rasping breath, I saw his lineaments

heard him chase me down corridors of loss
which end in blank walls of granite,
reading the adverts for stonemasons
in the air-conditioned funeral parlour.

And I heard political wizardry swear black
was white and that denying one or other
was not a racial matter, and how a sticky web
of information would save the world

though there's no one left to say which
clever formula is right or wrong
it's the appearance that is all the
interactive, hypertextual, death

infinitely preferable to the stinking body
teeth-bared on some bloody pavement
the ants already at their summer task
scurrying between the palate and the tongue.

The black prince lies murdered in another
coup, while folks are line-dancing towards
the apocalypse, all in step, ignoring the
baroque variations of suffering that make

our pleasures possible. After all this
what is left for the next year and the next?
An ambition to listen more closely to silence
after music, score out another line or two?

FIN DE SIÈCLE

Clouds swirl sunset colours
through the blue;
at the end of this century
it's fairy floss,
bubble-gum ice cream we see:
an advert for a spree.

Having eaten the sky
we can look forward
to another hoarding
which encourages us
to gulp the dark,
chewing hard on icy shards
that once romantic poets called
the moon and stars.